Careers in Sport

your questions and answers

TROTMAN

This first edition published in 1995 in Great Britain by Trotman and Company Limited, 12 Hill Rise, Richmond, Surrey TW10 6UA

British Library Cataloguing in Publication Data

A catalogue record for this book is available from the British Library

ISBN 0 85660 253 1

Printed and bound in Great Britain

Contents

What about working in sport?

The world of sport is a large and growing industry. It is a part of an even larger employment sector, that of leisure, which has developed from non-existent in the 1960s and 1970s to one that employs 400,000 people in the 1990s in sports alone. The most visible sign in the huge growth in sport as a leisure activity is the increasing number of high street sports clubs and gyms. In the 1970s there were only 20 sports centres in the UK, now there are 1500.

The careers available are also increasing in number and diversity. These careers now embrace professional sport, coaching, teaching physical education, sports centre management, grounds keeping as well as outdoor pursuits. Not only are more people playing sports, they no longer practise just in the evenings or weekends. Nor do they stick to the same old sports as they used to do. Brand new or little known sports are developing strong followings from dedicated fans, and this trend is set to continue.

As the UK comes out of the worst recession since the Second World War, the opportunities will be even greater. People will have more to spend on their chosen sports, there will be more prize money for certain events, more sponsorship, more TV coverage from cable and satellite channels. The future looks good.

What is the difference between amateur and professional?

It is important to be clear about this. Professional does not just mean expert and amateur, not so expert. The basic difference between the two is that the professional sports player is paid directly by his or her club, whilst the amateur is not. Most sports beyond a certain level of involvement can become professional. Cricket players who play at county or national team level are professional, the rest are amateur. Footballers in the Premier, First and Second Divisions are paid, as well as some, but not all, Third Division and Vauxhall Conference players.

Although most sports are professional, some remain strictly amateur, even though they may have a high profile. One of these is athletics; no matter how good a sprinter or javelin-thrower you are you will not be paid for performing. A few sports are semi-professional. Boxers, for example, may or may not be paid. Rugby League is a professional sport, whereas the slightly different Rugby Union is wholly amateur. Don't think, however, that top amateur sports players cannot benefit financially from their prowess. The distinction is not being paid directly to perform: but there is nothing to stop a amateur being sponsored by a company, where the player will wear a company's logo. Sometimes whole teams are sponsored. Beefeater Gin invests heavily in the strictly amateur Oxford and Cambridge Boat Race teams, and will pay for boats, uniforms and a professional coach.

Things are further complicated by the fact that some amateurs spend all their time training, whilst some professionals have a second job. A second team player in a football club will not be paid enough to survive on without working in a factory or office or whatever, full-time. He will train outside normal nine-to-five hours. A golf-course will employ a 'pro', a professional golfer who not only represents his club, but will also be required to coach other players as well as give advice on equipment, or work in the club shop.

For the purposes of this book however, when 'professional' sports players are referred to, this means those who are at the forefront of their sport, whether they are paid or not.

How do people work in sport?

For the lucky few who become professional (or highly successful amateur) players, sport is a very rewarding occupation. But, as will be described, even if you do reach the top, you are unlikely to be there for long. So if sport is to be your career for life, actually playing may only be a small part of what you might end up doing in the industry. Many people working in sports and leisure have other types of jobs which do not necessarily involve competitive play, such as coaching, fitness training or administration in clubs, sports and leisure centres or activity centres – and opportunities in these areas are increasing all the time. Teaching in a school, teaching dance or fitness in an evening class or helping people with disabilities to enjoy sporting activities are also highly rewarding occupations which will keep you, as well as those you are helping, in good shape. Specialist areas of work such as treating sports injuries, or succeeding in sports journalism, are also possible careers. There is a good range of jobs in the industry as will be outlined in the next two sections.

What sorts of jobs are there?

Active, player jobs in sport, as has been described, tend to be limited, short term and amateur on the whole, but the opportunities nevertheless will vary across the many different sports available. If you have been lucky enough to have had support and been able to develop your potential in one particular activity, such as horse riding, ballet or motor sport, for example, you could go on to greater things in the longer term.

Among the many non-competing jobs in the industry, however, there is a whole range of different occupations. Some of the more common ones will be found in these broad areas:

Coaching

Many coaches in various sports are ex-players themselves and this is a rewarding area of work for those keen to stay on the competitive side. The opportunities at top level (ie full-time, paid jobs) are limited, however .

Teaching sport

Teaching sport and PE in a school is one of the options available if you are keen to help others develop their potential. You will need degree level qualifications for this, however (see page 10). You might also consider teaching fitness or various sports at evening classes for which other, less demanding (ie in terms of years spent training), qualifications might be appropriate (see page 43).

Turf accounting and hospitality work

A large number of people are employed in betting shops and on race courses across the country. Horse racing is the sport most obviously associated with this area, however, so if you are keen to become involved in this sport, learning to be a turf accountant might be one way you can do so.

Promotional and hospitality work connected with various sports has become another growth area in recent years, with many companies both sponsoring competitions and major annual events and offering their employees bonuses in the form of tickets to see top occasions in the sporting calendar – such as Wimbledon, or the Test matches. Although jobs in this area are harder to obtain, if you aim to work for a company with a high profile in sport (or a PR or travel company which specialises in such work) you could succeed via this route.

Sports journalism

You could train as a journalist either straight from school or as a graduate (see page 43) and aim to specialise in sport as you go along, although you will have to learn the basics of journalism across much wider areas than just sport to begin with. Based with a local newspaper, national newspaper or TV or radio station as a sports reporter, commentator or camera operator, there are opportunities for keen and talented people in this popular area of journalism though the competition to get to the top, once again, is strong.

Recreation management

As recently as 1970 this profession didn't exist as such. There were only about 20 sports centres in the whole country, now there are more than 1500. They all need trained staff to manage and run them, from administrators to managers, to supervisory staff, such as swimming pool attendants and lifeguards. They all help towards making sure a facility, indoor or outdoor, is run efficiently and safely. Competition in this area is intense; you would do well to apply for BTEC, City and Guilds or even degree/HND courses (see page 42).

Grounds keeping

Expertly and safely maintained pitches and other facilities are vital. After all, a cricket match can be altered radically by slight variations in the condition of a few square yards of pitch. It is an important job, albeit one that players and spectators very rarely consider. They probably assume the grass is kept immaculate by magic! It is a highly skilled, outdoor job, working in all weathers. Without the grounds keeper's art and skill many more fixtures would be cancelled. There is a general shortage of experienced grounds keepers. Most start as a parks worker for a local council. Check your local paper and the Jobcentre in the spring. You can then progress slowly to being a 'crafts grounds keeper' either through courses or through on-the-job training.

Sports medicine

This area of medicine has advanced by leaps and bounds over the last 15 years. As sport is seen as more important than it once was, and since more people are taking part, there are more and more opportunities in this field. There are three main types of sports medical specialists – doctors, physiotherapists and osteopaths. Doctors will treat sports injuries, although few will deal only with sports cases. (Obviously, training for a medical career is extremely demanding, both in terms of years at university and in terms of academic ability; few would use this as a route into sports-related work.)
Physiotherapists are experts in how the body moves, and how the muscles, joints, ligaments and tendons interact. They will prescribe exercises or other treatments to accelerate the healing process after an injury. Osteopathy, while still not recognised by the National Health Service, is increasingly popular. It is another method of manipulating joints and bones to promote recovery after an injury. For all three disciplines you will need to qualify first, and then choose to specialise in sport. There are few opportunities to concentrate exclusively on sports injuries and many people who assist at clubs' games, who may have first aid qualifications or knowledge of sports massage techniques, often volunteer for the work. But there are such qualifications available for those keen to increase their skills (see page 42).

Where will I work? Large or small employers?

Sports fields	–	*Football, hockey, cricket, grounds keeping, field athletics*
Sports centres	–	*Keep-fit, aerobics, weight-training, administration*
Gymnasiums	–	*Dance, gymnastics*
Outdoor pursuits centres	–	*Orienteering, canoeing, mountain biking*
Rivers, streams, lakes	–	*Rowing, angling, water-skiing*
At sea	–	*Sailing, wind surfing, power boating*
Mountains and cliffs	–	*Mountaineering, hang-gliding, climbing*
Underwater	–	*Scuba-diving, octopush (underwater polo)*
Swimming pools	-	*Water polo, swimming, lifeguards*
In the air	–	*Gliding, parachuting, ballooning*
Martial arts' dojos	–	*Karate, judo*
Courts indoor/outdoor	–	*Lawn and real tennis, badminton,squash, netballoutdoor/indoor*

Schools and hospitals	–	*Teaching, therapy work in sports*
On ice	–	*Ice Hockey, ice and figure skating, bobsleigh*
On horseback	–	*Polo, horse-racing, dressage, show-jumping*
On sand	–	*Petanque, long jump*
Ranges	–	*Archery, rifle-shooting*
Tracks	–	*Running, high-jump*
Tables	–	*Snooker, billiards, table tennis*
Snow	–	*Skiing, snow surfing*
Underground	–	*Cave-diving, pot-holing*
Ring	–	*Boxing, wrestling*
Lawn	–	*Croquet, Bowls*
On the road/circuits	–	*Roller-skating, cycling, motor-racing, auto sports*
Courses	–	*Golf*
Parks	–	*Softball, rounders*
Stadiums	–	*Speedway, greyhound racing*
Sports retailers	–	*Sales and marketing work, turf accountant*
TV studios or newspaper office	–	*Sports journalists, camera operators and photographers*

What size are the various organisations?

There are few really big sporting organisations. A big football or cricket club may employ 40 or even 50 people, including players, coaches, managers, grounds-keepers amongst others, but most places of sport are far smaller. Indeed a large sports centre may be run by a staff of just ten or so; most clubs are run with lots of volunteers helping in their spare time. Many people just want to play a sport – they don't need supervision or coaching. Even governing bodies are run by a mere handful of full-time staff.

What qualifications will I need?

Players As a young full-time football trainee, your club will require you to keep up with your studies. The worst possible situation is to be dropped by a club without qualifications (academic or not), work experience, or a trade to fall back on. You can choose between day-release courses, GCSEs and A-levels, or learn a practical skill like brick-laying or engineering. It is vital for all sports players, in whatever sport, to have a second string to their bow. Your career could end at 16, 23, 31 or any other time before or after and you simply will not get a job on the strength of your sporting talents alone. You have to have something else to offer.

Many players think very little about this. Their minds, naturally enough, are focused on their careers. However, you should bear in mind that even famous football players have ended up as milkmen or window-cleaners or on the dole. The end of a professional sporting career is devastating enough; unless you have at least some other prospects, it will be even worse.

Teachers All sports teachers have to have recognised qualifications. In the case of Physical Education teachers, a degree from a university or college of higher education is required and there are two main routes. Students can study for a BEd (Bachelor of Education). The course will last three or four years full-time. Alternatively they can study a non-related course (Geology, French, Chemistry etc) and follow this by a one-year, full-time course known as a PGCE

(Postgraduate Certificate of Education). To do a PGCE you must be a graduate. To do a first degree, whether it is a BEd or not, you will need five GCSE passes and two or three A-level passes or their equivalent. Obviously an interest in sport is also essential. If you are absolutely sure you want to be a teacher then a BEd is your best bet, as it will save you time, whilst giving you excellent qualifications. If you are not absolutely sure, you can keep your options open by doing another degree such as a BA or BSc. This may have an element of sport or sports teaching built into it. You can then gain the necessary specific qualifications by doing a PGCE and perhaps a fitness training certificate so that you can teach sport in addition to another subject.

Coaches The qualifications you will need as a coach are issued by the appropriate governing body. Each governing body has its own award scheme, which provides training for coaches at all levels. While formal qualifications are required, much can profitably be learned from watching experienced coaches at work. Don't forget that much of the job is experience – knowing how people think, how they will react, knowing when to push them and when to hold them back. These aspects can't really be taught in classrooms.

One way to speed up the transition from amateur to professional coach is to take the Diploma in Professional Studies (Sports Coaching) at Heriot Watt University (in Edinburgh). This is a one-year full-time course and is available to all who have an established record in coaching, either paid or unpaid.

Sports centres administration For those who want to succeed as managers in the sports and leisure industry there are degree courses available. But there are many other administrative qualifications available which would enable you to work in a sports centre on the non-competitive side (see page 43).

What skills and attitudes are needed?

If you are looking to play a sport you will need great talent – outstanding talent that is not even close to reaching its full potential yet. You will need to be head and shoulders above the others in your year – being good is not enough. You will also need to possess a certain amount of luck!

Apart from physical abilities you will also need to have a certain temperament – with a determination to work extremely hard, day-in and day-out, even when other people are off on holiday or relaxing with their friends.

As a PE teacher you will need to be able to relate to children of different age groups. Not only will you have to maintain discipline, you will also need to be able to motivate your team and individual players. It is a job that requires a great deal of patience, as well as stamina.

While PE teachers will teach a variety of the more common sports to children, a coach will work with people of all ages, teaching them usually just one sport, certainly at the higher levels. Here you will need endless enthusiasm as well as a thorough understanding of your chosen sport. The job also calls for motivation, leadership and organisational skills. A coach needs to be able to inspire his or her trainees and impart the right attitude as well as teaching them how to use a golf club, cricket bat, hockey stick or racquet.There are common skills and attitudes needed for all those involved in sport. As well as concern for safety, competitors and trainers alike need to be optimistic and not discouraged by defeats and poor performances. Perseverance, the ability to keep, going goes hand-in-hand with this.

How do I get into this work?

To become a professional sports player you have to be seen in action by the right people. If you're lucky, the coach or teacher of your school team will have good contacts with the people who select or choose those who play in teams representing your district, borough or county in whatever sport.

Entry into a town's home team or county team is a good way of attracting the attention of potential employers. However, if your school coach does not know who to ask, or is not interested in you playing at a higher level, contact the secretary of the regional branch of your sport's governing body. Every sport has its own governing body. For cricket it is the National Cricket Association, for football, the Football Association, for athletics, the Amateur Athletics Association, and so on (see page 47). There are over 200 of them. Once you have found out from them the names and addresses of the district or county selector(s), ask your coach or parents to invite one of them to see you play. It is important to give a choice of dates.

Another good way to promote your sports abilities is to join a local club which plays your particular sport. Many of these have junior sections and will help you to fulfil your potential by coaching you and offering matches against other clubs. It is at these club matches where you start to show what you are capable of. Your school sports teacher may be able to recommend a good club, or again contact the regional branch of your sport's governing body. Selectors regularly visit the better sports clubs looking for new talent. If you are particularly good you will be noticed and the next step in the ladder to a paid career will be open to you. From this point on career paths are different for different sports.

For those interested in working in the sports industry at a non-competitive level, the qualifications outlined on pages 10 and 42 are the most likely routes to success.

What should I do now to prepare?

If you want to do more than shine in your best sport at school, you will need to make sacrifices and posses great determination and competitiveness. As described in the last section, various sports bodies may be able to assist with your training and progress. Two of the most popular options are, however, football and cricket.

Football Most boys who end up playing in the Football League have been signed up by a club by the time they are 14. They will be signed up as Associated Schoolboys, usually for a year. This means they will train with the club for two or three evening sessions a week, after school. At 16, the club may or may not decide to sign you as a full-time trainee, on a two-year Youth Training Scheme contract. You will have to leave school and may have to leave home if the club is a long way off. On top of playing and training you will have to do chores, such as cleaning and checking kit and sweeping the changing rooms.

The real test comes at 18: you will either be taken on full-time or dropped from your club. Obviously only the very best of the best succeed at this level.

Cricket There are only about 350 professional cricketers, employed by 17 professional county clubs. This is done by being recommended by your school or club coach. The most talented players are put forward for trials, at age groups from under 11 to under 19. The best players will be selected for their county school XI and the best of the best, the 'top guns' so to speak, will go on to play for their county's second XI. Those selected are usually, but not always, from the older age ranges. Many players will get to play for the second team: there is still a very wide gap between this and the first team. The vast majority of second XI players are part-time. The team functions as a kind of proving ground from which the top few will be selected to play for the first XI. Remember though that county cricket is not a rich sport, and that being given a contract depends not only on your skills but also on how much money a club has to spend.

A word of caution

If you are offered the chance to sign with a football, cricket, rugby or any other sort of club – congratulations. But do think very carefully before signing any contract. Talk it through with your parents. Ask someone from your prospective club to talk to them so that both you and your parents know fully what you are letting yourself in for. For example, as an Associated Schoolboy linked to a particular club, you won't be able to play for any other club. As an assistant Professional Golfer (or 'Pro') you won't be able to compete in amateur tournaments. You may also need the permission of your school Headteacher. Make sure you get it. An offer from the top football or cricket club, among others, sounds perfect. But remember that they take on more young hopefuls than smaller clubs and so there is a greater chance of being dropped. Don't turn your nose up at smaller or less successful professional clubs. You can always change clubs once you have established yourself.

What are the good and bad aspects of the work?

The challenges

Whilst some top sports players – athletes, show-jumpers or golfers, for example – have wonderful lifestyles that the rest of us can merely envy, it has to be remembered that these lucky few are very few indeed. There are many thousands of sportsmen and women who never reach the top, either because of lack of opportunity or ability or because of injury. Those who do reach the top have done so on account of very hard work and some luck too!

There's no relaxing once you're at this peak. No matter how gifted a sports player, such is the professionalism current nowadays, you will have to work very hard to stay there. Players are under enormous pressure to perform consistently well, all the time. Ordinary mortals can have good and bad days. Not so professional sports players. There is always the fear lurking at the back of their minds that someone better, more talented, fitter, will come along and replace them in the team. So to stay on top sportsmen and women need unwavering dedication and commitment.

A coach, whilst requiring similar qualities, also needs to be able to take a backseat role once his or her team or trainees are exercising their skills in competition. It is a fact of life that during training a coach works long and hard honing their skills. On the day of the big event if their trainees do well, they, and not the coach, will get all the glory. Few will stop to think where the credit really lies. If the trainees don't do well, team managers, maybe even an individual player, can be apt to blame the coach. A coach's job isn't over even when the trainee has gone for a shower. He or she will have to evaluate each day's training, and work out what else needs to be done.

The rewards

Sport plays a major part in many of our lives. Who hasn't dreamed of scoring the winning goal in football, or edging past other sprinters to break the finishing-tape first, even those who are merely 'armchair sports fans' watching it on TV. In the summer, Wimbledon or the Test Match can excite even those not normally interested in these sports.

Those who enjoy the greatest success in the field of sports careers, the top sportsmen and women, are national figures or even national heroes who may be paid huge sums of money and appear on TV – all for doing something they love. In spite of the difficulties and the intense, constant competition, someone has to race Formula One cars, or play cricket for England: why not you?

With luck and the right abilities your sporting prowess could set you up for life. Properly invested, your earnings could last a lifetime, bearing in mind a professional career could last ten years or more. Furthermore, if you can learn other skills, it could also be a great starting point to employment in business, or in sports administration, recreation management, show business – you name it!

Any job in sport is likely to keep you young in body, young at heart, fit and healthy. Few jobs in this sector are sedentary – ie purely sitting down. You will also be surrounded by fit, keen young people and their enthusiasm is infectious. Teaching, whether as a PE teacher at school, or as an aerobics instructor in a fitness centre is rewarding. Slowly, but steadily, you can see your charges learning new skills or reaching their potential.

Sport is meant to be fun and enjoyable. Unlike purely academic subjects like Maths or French, which relatively fewer people enjoy, the games teacher should have less of a problem motivating his or her pupils and keeping them interested than other teachers. For many school children (though not all), PE is their favourite lesson. They enjoy the chance to tax their bodies rather than their minds!

Who will I work with?

A career in sport will give you the opportunity to work alongside people who share your interest in and passion for sport. They are likely to be young, fit, enthusiastic, motivated. The atmosphere tends to be relaxed and informal. Even at the very top levels, stress and tension are not conducive to a good sporting performance. The kind of people you deal with and work alongside is what gives a career in sport its very satisfying quality of life. It is these people and the bonds you form with them that will allow you to cope with the often low pay and long, irregular hours.

What will I earn?

While a professional sports player's earning potential can be very high, this is only true in certain sports at the top level – cricket, golf, football, tennis, motor-racing, boxing or basketball among others. Indeed in many sports, no matter how good you are you will never earn enough to live on. You will have to have a second job. Very few Rugby League players, for example, can do so. In tennis, unless you are good enough to play nationally you will never make a living from this game. What's more, at the beginning of your professional career you may find yourself relying on your parents for financial support or a roof over your head. This is especially true in tennis where you will have to pay part of your accommodation and travel costs when competing in tournaments. An Assistant Golf Pro may be paid no more than £70 a week. In this case you will almost certainly have to live with your parents until you progress to a higher level.

In all sports, whilst you may end up earning fabulous sums, you will certainly start off your professional career earning very little. Consider football, which is generally the best paid. As a young trainee you will earn around £40 a week, plus travel or lodging allowance and possibly a share of the 'win bonus' scheme. At 18 you will be paid at least £100 a week. If you are promoted to the first team, playing before the big crowds and the TV cameras, you will earn a great deal more. The salary of a Premier league player is at least £1700 a week!

Cricketers are not so well paid. While Test match players will be paid around £1800 or so per game, a 20 year-old player will only be paid around £6000 for the whole season.

There are other sources of income. Sponsors either sponsor a player or will put up the prize money for a particular event. Although this usually goes into the club's coffers, some of it will filter down to the players. There is also the possibility of income through endorsing and advertising products, or by appearing as a celebrity guest on TV or in real life, opening a supermarket or giving after dinner speeches.

A PE teacher's salary is more modest, but also more secure. The salary differs according to various factors, one of which is where in the country you teach. Inner London is paid the most, followed by Outer London, followed by the rest of the country. The least you will be paid is £13,000 per annum. It might very well be several thousand pounds more once you have a few years' experience behind you.

A coach's pay, when they are paid at all, varies hugely. The best paid are team coaches at national and international level. Often the worst paid full-time professional coaches are outdoor pursuits instructors. While they receive accommodation and food free of charge, on the other hand their actual salary can be little more than pocket money. Full-time jobs in leisure or sports centre management are likely to be more secure and better paid but the rates vary according to level of responsibility and local authority rates of pay; from under £10,000 to over £20,000 pa.

What are the hours and holidays like?

There are few jobs in the world of sports that do not involve working long, often irregular hours. Many professional sports players have to share facilities with the public. They normally gear their practice times to when the public are not around so they can benefit from the peace and quiet and concentrate wholly on their training. Ice-skaters, swimmers and the like will therefore need to get up very early to use these facilities before they are open to the general public. Others like footballers, cricketers and rugby players don't have these constraints, but they still train long and hard. Most amateur sports players must practise in their spare time, including obviously at weekends, or during holidays from their normal working routine. Professional players may have some paid leave, but this will be strictly controlled by their club's seasonal programme and their training regime.

Coaches' hours at the very highest levels are even longer than those they train. Not only will they have to be with the players while they train, but they will also need to spend time checking and evaluating equipment as well as working out training and diet programmes. At other levels, coaches will obviously need to work when their trainees aren't at work or at school. They will tend to work in the evenings and also at weekends, which can be hard on their families and social life. Indoor coaches can work longer hours than those based outdoors, such as sailing coaches or those who instruct at outdoor pursuits centres. These coaches will obviously be limited by the number of daylight hours.

Non-teaching staff at leisure and sports centres – such as managers, deputy managers, life guards – often work shifts. Remember these places are often open from around seven in the morning to nine or ten in the evening, seven days a week. The hours they work will vary from day to day and week to week but they would normally expect a minimum of four weeks' holiday each year (if they are employed on a permanent contract).

All school teachers work long hours; the difference between PE teachers and other teachers is that while the former will be marking homework outside lesson hours, the PE teacher will be organising clubs at lunchtime, team practice in the evening and attending and refereeing school matches at weekends. They also have more paperwork and administration to do than they used to. On the other hand most PE teachers greatly enjoy their work, so they can put up with the long hours. Teachers usually receive more paid holiday than people working in other careers. For PE teachers who might be involved in a sport personally, the holidays are often a chance for them to practise or play on tour.

Will I meet the public?

Almost certainly, if you consider the public simply as 'other people'; very few sports, even those done on an individual basis, are undertaken alone. A possible exception is hang-gliding! It is important to have others around. Not only is it more fun, you will need help from others if you become injured or get into trouble in any way.

If on the other hand, by 'the public' is meant people who come to see you perform as a competitor the answer is both yes and no. On the one hand they will see you (since that is the whole object of the exercise!) and you will see them. On the other hand you won't really meet them unless you specifically choose to do so, since they will be kept away from the areas of play.

The one major exception to meeting the public is the grounds keeper. They do their job before the public arrive. Not only will the public not see or meet the keeper, most of them will be blissfully unaware he or she has put a great deal of work into a pitch. All they will see will be the end result, not all the hard work it took.

What insights will this work give me?

Life, like sport, is competitive. We all have to compete for jobs, for a partner, for a decent place to live. However, we also live as a society, which means we have to rely on each other. No-one on their own could provide or produce everything he or she needs : transport, food, housing, clothing, education, health and welfare services, entertainment. We have to help each other and respect each other by abiding by written and unwritten rules. As in society, so in sport. A sports team has to work together to succeed. An individual sports player, for example a golfer, although on his/her own, nevertheless needs to obey the rules.

Thus the key insight sport offers is how we react to and how to promote co-operation and discipline. Since sport can be seen as a reflection of society, these attributes learnt on the sports field, are readily transferable to society as a whole. Socially useful skills, such as a sense of fair play and the recognition that rules can ultimately be of benefit to everyone (as long as everyone abides by them!) can thus be learnt in an enjoyable and natural way.

The Victorians were very enthusiastic towards sport as a character-building exercise. After a long decline, this thinking is starting to come back into fashion. The importance of promoting health and fitness is just one aspect. For even in so-called 'uncompetitive' sports like hang-gliding or mountaineering we are competing against ourselves. When we do well we feel a real sense of achievement, which goes a long way towards promoting a positive outlook.

Sport has been described as a form of sanitised warfare, with each side struggling against the other for victory. The higher the level of competition, the clearer and stronger are the strains of victory and defeat. At the top levels, mental attitude and psychology are almost as important as physical prowess. It is vital for a coach, amateur or professional, to understand how people's minds work in order to motivate his or her trainees effectively and keep their sense of commitment strong.

What about training at work?

Professional sports players are constantly 'training', with the help of their coaches, to improve their abilities, skills and/or speeds in their respective sports. Career development training, however, varies a great deal in non-participant jobs in the sports industry and depends, to a large extent, on the size of the employer. A sports centre with a number of staff may have a policy of training whereby staff can gain further qualifications to achieve promotion and/or learn new skills. In other specialised areas of sports it is very difficult to generalise about the type of training which might help improve a person's career, be it in management or business skills, knowledge of anatomy (eg for sports injuries or for sports research), diet, fitness training, career development for teachers, and so on. Often people who work for smaller employers or individual clubs, especially those sports organisations with a limited amount of funds available, must try and improve their skills and employment prospects by attending courses in their own time and at their own expense (though often employers will allow some time off for job-related training). Examples of some of the different qualifications are given on pages 42-43.

What are the recent developments in this area?

Leisure is now a huge industry. Until the late 1970s the word meant no more than time not spent at work. Not only is it now a very important employment sector, but it is still growing fast . It caters for all those who wish to spend their free time in some way organised by others. Sport is the largest single part of the leisure industry and has grown with it. This is shown by the boom in sports centres, the keep fit and aerobics industry, specialist sports clubs and others.

One of the reasons more sport is being played is that people are retiring earlier than they used to. Employees are also getting more annual holiday. There are also a large number of unemployed people who use their time to practise sport. All this means that sport is now being played seven days a week, and not just in the evenings and at weekends.

Companies are becoming increasingly keen to promote sports playing among their staff. It makes very good sense. They recognise that a fit, healthy workforce is happier and likely to take fewer days off through sickness. A department that plays a team sport together is also apt to communicate better in the workplace. Large companies, by having their own private sports facilities, make themselves more attractive to potential employees. All companies, no matter how bad the recession, have to work hard to attract and keep top quality staff. Even those without their own facilities are keen to organise a squash ladder or a netball team which competes against other companies in a league.

Sport is also becoming more and more diverse. People are taking up more unusual sports. There are new sports to be played like Octopush (a form of underwater polo) and Korfball. Other sports have been imported from overseas. Softball, which originated in the USA, is now gaining popularity in Britain. All this is because people want to try out something different. Old prejudices and divisions are being broken down. Golf used to be seen as a recreation for the wealthy few. Not any more. The English Golf Union, the governing body of golf in England, reports that if demand for the sport continues to be as strong as it is at present, not dozens, but hundreds of new courses will need to be built. Another example is Rugby League which used to be played just in the North of England. Now there is a Rugby League club in London, the London Broncos, and with new sponsorship on the horizon, the sport looks set to increase in popularity in future.

The bottom line is that increased demand for sporting facilities means that more are being built or provided – whether by companies for their own employees, private companies specialising in sport, or local or national government. There are more employment opportunities each year.

Opportunities for women in sport?

Sporting competitions have traditionally been divided between men and women – eg in athletics or tennis. There are few sports where women compete against men. One exception to this is in the world of horses, where there are a growing number of women jockeys and showjumpers. But women are now competing more widely in sports which were once only played by men, such as cricket, football and Rugby Union.

However, some sports continue to offer competition at the highest levels for men only, such as boxing or motor racing. Even the superlative sportswoman who is good enough to deserve a place in a male team and who may be the best available player can be barred and so cannot experience the highest level of competition. Men's events are, wrongly, usually seen as more prestigious, and so are better sponsored and carry higher prize money than women's. This means more male events are televised than women's and men get more attention in the press and radio as well.

On the brighter side, the situation is improving slowly. Athletics is one example where women like Sally Gunnell and Liz McColgan have become an inspiration for young, would-be champions. More all-female teams are being created in traditionally masculine sports and leagues are being formed so that they can compete with each other. Furthermore, at a national level, the women's teams often do better than their male counterparts. In certain sports the gap is narrowing between male and female achievements; tennis is an example of this. Spectators have realised that women's tennis is as enjoyable to watch as men's.

All this means that potential sportswomen should not feel discouraged and should not be dissuaded from professional sport as a career. All the signs are that women in sport will continue slowly to get a better and better deal.

Will I need other languages for the work?

The ability to speak languages other than English is always useful, but is rarely essential for the majority of jobs. However, many sports are becoming increasingly internationalised and often top-level players may find themselves working in another European country, at least for a few months, or for a season. The ability to converse in the language of the host country will obviously be useful, and for sports players, and athletes who attend international events on a frequent basis, especially where results may be broadcast in another language, comprehension may be a distinct advantage.

For other types of work it is difficult to generalise. You might find, as someone involved in marketing for a large sports equipment manufacturer, for example, that fluency in other languages is a plus. You might even work for an international sports organisation where this would become essential. But on the whole, work in sports is likely to be mainly UK-based.

Will I be able to work overseas or travel for my job?

It is in the very nature of things that sports players compete. The very best will not just meet each other in this country but will also go abroad for matches, tournaments etc. The schedules can be punishing, however, and you are unlikely to have either the time or the inclination to see much of the lands you visit. You are, after all, there to do a job and you will have to focus your energies on the competition.

A sports teacher does have the option of getting a job abroad. With the advent of the single European market a qualified PE teacher or ski instructor does not need a work permit to work in any EU country. The opportunities are there.

The same is true for coaching. Proper qualifications and a proven, successful track record – maybe even a diploma from a university – are widely recognised over much of the world. High quality, dedicated, professional coaches don't grow on trees. A foreign team or individual athlete will have no qualms hiring a Briton if they can't find exactly what they want in their own country.

Will I use computers in this work?

If you work in a sports or leisure centre you will find that computers are used quite widely, both in office-based word processing and accounting systems, and computerised booking systems in reception areas for membership details, and for the reservation of facilities. For those involved in research, perhaps in a university sports science department or for a national sports organisation, you may become involved in work which is more computer-based in content. Computers are making inroads into so many areas, some of which may be related to sport – such as broadcasting, timing devices, and various types of training equipment – that few sports environments are likely to be free of computer technology altogether. However, for the majority of sports-related jobs which are not office-based, computers are less likely to be used.

Could I become famous?

As a professional sports player you are likely to be seen exercising your skills by a crowd of people. Having said that, not all sports attract large crowds. Even those that do, like football or motor racing, will only do so at the highest levels. Cricket matches, even at county level, may have audiences numbered in hundreds rather than thousands. This success does not necessarily equal fame, although the two are linked. It all depends how popular is your particular sport. You could be the small-bore Rifle Shooting World Champion, yet still not be as famous as a merely average British Formula One racing driver.

The key is television. The more a particular sport is watched live by spectators who are actually there, the more this sport will be televised, and thus the more interest will be generated in its top participants. Many of the best-known names come from football, our national sport. It has the largest number of spectators, both at the match, and watching it on TV. However, even here only the most important matches are televised – ie those between premier league teams and some in the first division, apart from international matches. Even then, often only the highlights are shown.

Cricket and rugby similarly are only shown live for international matches, and even then not all of a test match will be available on TV. Most major spectator sports do appear to a certain extent on TV, even if only for a half hour or so.

The thing to remember is that all fame is relative. A mere dozen or so household names like Paul Gascoigne or Tessa Sanderson will be known to more or less everyone. The further down you are from the peak of your sport, the more likely you are to be known only by those who take a keen interest in your sport at national or local level. Even a Vauxhall conference football player will be known only to those who support his team – week in, week out.

Remember, however, that fame is a two-edged sword. When you are playing well, everyone thinks you're a hero. But you only have to make one mistake for that fame to become a burden, when everyone criticises you and thinks you're useless. Nor can all those who achieve fame handle the constant attention, constant analysis and probing in their private lives.

One way in which fame is always a bonus is in the matter of sponsorship. The better your face and name is known, the more potential sponsors will see you as a 'hot property'. An individual competitor has the advantage over a team player here.

A coach or PE teacher will be known and respected only throughout his or her club or school. The coach of even a famous gymnast is unlikely to get much of the limelight. All eyes will be on the star pupil.

Could I work independently?

Not if you're part of a sports team. The person who tries to go it alone will be held in very low esteem by his or her fellow team members. Even individual competitors will have their coach with them.

There are, however, definite possibilities. All teachers in a sense work independently from other adults most of the time and have some autonomy – people rarely learn effectively from two people both trying to teach at the same time. Yet the PE teacher will be even more 'alone' than his or her academic colleagues and is less likely to be surrounded by other classrooms, probably having more space to operate in. That is one of the great rewards of any teaching job in sport. You're your own boss. Within a fairly broad set of rules you do more or less what you want, how you want.

The same applies to grounds keepers. As long as the facilities are ready for use come Saturday or whenever, you can go about your preparation as you see fit, rather than just obeying other people. So while there are few opportunities for freelance work in sport – except perhaps those in sports journalism and photography – there are some jobs which give a measure of autonomy.

What other considerations are there?

Safety

Many sports are potentially dangerous. This is often part and parcel of the thrill and excitement of a sport. Apart from such things as golf, bowls or snooker, sport, unless carefully supervised and controlled, can be a danger to players or spectators. Of course some sports are inherently more dangerous than others. Motor racing is more dangerous than cross country running. The safety considerations therefore vary from sport to sport. A tennis player only has to make sure he or she is properly warmed up, thus minimising pulled or torn ligaments and damaged joints. A rugby referee has to check boots for dangerous studs as well as being constantly aware of the dangers to players at the bottom of a collapsed scrum, for example, as well as penalising high tacklers.

Governing bodies spend a lot of time and effort doing all that can be done to make sport as safe as possible, by changing the rules or stipulating safety equipment or protective clothing. They will insist that qualified coaches are trained in first aid.

Children and novices are particularly vulnerable. Instructors have to be aware of this at all times and check that everything is as safe as possible and used correctly: footwear, equipment, playing facilities, etc. Teachers and referees have a vital duty in this respect. The players are totally in their hands and they have to be confident in their trust.

What will I wear?

The single most likely piece of clothing is a track suit. With brightly coloured track-suits and casual wear now being popular off the sports field as well as on it, you could be the height of fashion! Although codes are fairly relaxed, you will be required to wear the appropriate clean kit, depending on what sport you are involved in.

You can normally tell what sport someone is playing just by what they wear. If you are particularly keen on wearing a grey suit and a sombre tie, or high heels and a tight skirt, this is perhaps not the industry for you!

Clothing is important in sport, not simply to distinguish one team from another, but also to maximise the body's capabilities (hence a sprinter's tight clothing, designed to cut down on wind resistance) but also to allow you to breathe and sweat naturally. Clothing also has very important safety considerations. If you go mountaineering you must wear a helmet; if sailing you must wear a life-jacket and so on.

How can I find out about the work?

Your careers teacher and/or local careers centre should be your first point of contact, as well as the books and magazines listed on pages 45-46. It may also be useful to obtain prospectuses from your local college of further education to see if there are any options available in sports or fitness-related work, or in other specialised skills such as grounds keeping or golf course management. If you wish to take a degree in Sports Science, PE Teaching or Leisure Management, or in the various sports-related therapies, there are several universities and colleges in the UK where this is possible: you should start by looking at some of their prospectuses as well as the higher education directories listed (which should also be available in your school or local library or careers centre).

For specific sports, the organisations listed on pages 47-50 will be able to help with advice, contacts and/or publications relating to their particular area of sporting interest, and there are a number of specialist magazines for the different sports.

Which courses and qualifications are available?

Degrees related to sports and leisure management vary between Sports Studies and Sports Science, Recreation Studies, Leisure Management and Turf Science. The content of the courses can vary substantially, from the more theoretical and scientific to the practical, participatory sports degrees where you will also spend some time training and competing in your particular sport. Some are more health-oriented than others. Degrees are taught at a number of universities and colleges of higher education across the UK and include the highly popular courses at Loughborough, one of the top universities for sport worldwide, and Roehampton Institute in South West London which specialises in Sports teaching degrees. There are several other universities and colleges of higher education where you can specialise in PE teaching or where you can take a PGCE with some sports content. For most degree courses, a minimum of two A-levels (or their equivalent in terms of Scottish Highers, GNVQ, BTEC and AS-levels) are required. For the more competitive courses, three A-levels (or equivalent) are specified. There are also some HND courses available in higher education, such as in Leisure Studies. Some useful guides to higher education are included in the booklist.

If you are interested in sports injuries as an area of work, you might decide to opt for this after a medical degree, but this requires high academic achievements (three science-based A-levels at high grades and their equivalent, plus good grades in a number of GCSEs), plus several years of hard training based in a hospital before you will even begin to specialise in sport. Physiotherapy is also a degree subject which is taught at several higher education institutions (contact the *Chartered Society of Physiotherapy*, 14 Bedford Row, London WC1R 4ED); Osteopathy is available through the British School of Osteopathy, 1-4 Suffolk Street, London SW1Y 4HG.

There are also certificate and diploma courses, taught at some colleges of further education in sports and health-related options. Examples are the IIST (International Institute of Sports Therapy) Diploma of Health and Fitness, the RSA (Royal Society of Arts) Exercise to Music and the NVQ (National Vocational Qualification) in International Health and Sports Therapy. These are designed for fitness trainers and people who want to work in a gym and include fitness techniques, sports massage and other aspects of health for sports. There are also some independent organisations which teach fitness certificates; the *YMCA* is one example.

If sports journalism is your goal you can opt for a media studies course at various levels – from BTEC diploma to degree level (find out which higher or further education institutions in your area might have courses) – or you can contact the *National Council for the Training of Journalists*, Latton Bush Business Centre, Southern Way, Harlow CM18 7BH.

There are also colleges which have departments teaching subjects related to horticulture and they may specialise in grounds work, golf course management and other sports and landscaping qualifications. On a more general level, training in aspects of business, management studies, accountancy and administration at various levels may become a useful way into working for a sports centre or large sports club on the administrative side.

Which organisations should I contact?

If you are interested in a particular sport, whether you are a beginner or someone who wants to try for a career as a professional player – or anything in between – you are advised to contact the respective governing body. Pages 47-50 lists a few of the bigger ones. If you write to them don't forget to include a stamped addressed envelope. Address your enquiry to the Secretary.

The list of sports bodies is just a selection – it is in no way complete. If the sport you are interested in is not listed, contact the Sports Council which is a sort of governing body for the governing bodies. Its head office is in London but it also has nine regional offices. Ask for the address of the one nearest you. For more advice on teaching PE as a career, speak to your careers officer or contact the Physical Education Association.

Vacancies are advertised in the local and national press (and particularly in *The Guardian* and the *Times Education Supplement*).

If you want to get into coaching and you are not sure where to start, contact the National Coaching Foundation. They produce Introductory Study Packs, as well as offer courses.

A good initial point of contact if you are interested in a career as a grounds-keeper is the Association of Playing Field Officers.

What publications should I look at?

Books and directories

A-Z of Careers and Jobs, Kogan Page, 1994.

Careers Encyclopaedia, Audrey Segal, Cassells, 1992.

Careers in Sport, Louis Fyfe, Kogan Page, 1994.

Careers in Teaching, Felicity Taylor, Kogan Page, 1992.

CRAC Directory of Further and Higher Education, Hobsons Publishing, Bateman Street, Cambridge CB2 1LZ

Degree Course Offers, Brian Heap, (annually updated) Trotman & Co Ltd, 12 Hill Rise, Richmond Surrey TW10 6UA.

Jobfile 95 – a compendium of job information, Cascaid,1994.

NATFHE Handbook, NATFHE

Penguin Careers Guide, Anne Alston & Anne Daniel, Penguin, 1993.

University and College Entrance, UCAS

Journals and newspapers

The daily newspapers; *The Sporting Life* specialises in horse racing news.

Magazines of interest to professionals working in sports and leisure centres and those connected with sports grounds include the following:

Horticulture Week (this includes sports grounds)

The Leisure Manager (monthly)

Leisure Week

Parks and Sports Grounds (monthly)

Sport and Leisure (bi-monthly), published by the Sports Council.

There are also dozens of different sports magazines and journals for different areas of sports specialism. The following weekly, monthly or bi-monthly are a (brief) selection: *Athletics Weekly*, *The Cricketer International*, *Cycling*, *Golf Weekly*, *Golf Monthly*, *The Good Ski Guide*, *Horse and Rider*, *Runner's World*, *Tennis World*, *Today's Golfer*, *Today's Runner*.

Some of the above may be available for reference in public libraries; most can be ordered through a newsagent.

Which addresses will help me?

Individual sports bodies

Athletics

Amateur Athletics Association of England
225a Bristol Road, Edgbaston, Birmingham B5 7UB
0121-440 5000

Badminton

Badminton Association of England
National Badminton Centre,Bradwell Road, Loughton Lodge
Milton Keynes, Buckinghamshire MK8 9LA
01908 568822

Basketball

English Basketball Association
48 Bradford Road, Stanningley, Leeds LS28 6DS
0113 236 1166

Boxing

Amateur Boxing Association
The National Sports Centre, Crystal Palace,London SE19 2BB
0181-778 0251

Cricket

National Cricket Association
Lords Cricket Ground,London NW8 8QN
0171-289 6098

Women's Cricket Association
Warwickshire County Cricket Ground
Edgbaston, Birmingham B5 7QX
0121-440 0520

Cycling

British Cycling Federation
Stuart Street, Manchester M11 4DQ
0161 223 2244

Football

Football Association
16 Lancaster Gate, London W2 3LW
0171-262 4542

Women's Football Association
9 Willyotts Place, Potters Bar, Herts EN6 2JD; 01707 651840

Golf

English Golf Union
1-3 Upper King Street, Leicester LE1 6XF; 0116 255 3042

English Ladies Golf Association
Edgbaston Golf Club, Church Road, Edgbaston,Birmingham B15 3TB
0121-456 2088

Gymnastics

British Amateur Gymnastics Association
Ford Hall, Lilleshall National Sports Centre, Newport,
Shropshire TF10 9ND
01952 820330

Hockey

All England Women's Hockey Association
51 High Street, Shrewsbury SY1 1ST
01743 233 572

The Hockey Associaiton
Norfolk House, 102 Saxon Gate West, Milton Keynes MK9 2EP
01908 241100

Judo

British Judo Association
7a Rutland Street, Leicester LE1 1RB
0116 559669

(Lawn) Tennis

Lawn Tennis Association
Queens Club, Barons Court, West Kensington, London W14 9EG
0171-385 2366

Martial Arts

Martial Arts Commission
Broadway House, 15-16 Deptford Broadway, London SE8 4PE
0181-691 3433

Mountaineering

British Mountaineering Council
177-179 Burton Road, West Didsbury, Manchester M20 2BB
0161-445 4747

Netball

All England Netball Association
Netball House, 9 Paynes Park, Hitchin, Herts SG5 1EH
01462 442344

Riding

British Horse Society
British Equestrian Centre, Stoneleigh, Kenilworth, Warwickshire CV8 2LR
01203 696697

Rugby League

British Amateur Rugby League Association
West Yorkshire House, 4 New North Parade, Huddersfield
West Yorkshire HD1 5JP
01484 544 131

Rugby Union

The Rugby Football Union,Whitton Road Twickenham
Middlesex TW1 1DX
0181-892 8161
Women's Rugby Football Union
Meadow House, Springfield Farm, Shipton-on-Stour
Warwickshire CV36 4HQ
01703 453371

Squash

Squash Rackets Association
Westpoint, Warple Way, Acton, London W3 ORQ
0181-746 1616

Swimming

Amateur Swimming Association
Harold Fern House, Derby Square, Loughborough
Leicestershire LE11 OAL
01509 230431

Table Tennis

English Table Tennis Association
Third Floor, Queensbury House, Havelock Road, Hastings
East Sussex TN34 1HF
01424 722525

Underwater Swimming

British Sub-Aqua Club
Telfords Quay, Ellesmere Port, South Wirral, Cheshire L65 4FY
0151-357 1951

General sports organisations

Association of Playing Field Officers
1 Cowley Road, Tuffley, Gloucestershire GL4 0HT
01452 425 355

National Coaching Foundation
114 Cardigan Road, Leeds LS6 3BJ
0113-274 4802

Physical Education Association
Francis House, Francis Street, London SW1P 1DE
0171-828 9229

The Sports Council
16 Upper Woburn Place, London WC1H 0QP; 0171-388 1277